THE UNTOLD SECRETS

Avis R. Waters

authorHOUSE®

AuthorHouse™
1663 Liberty Drive
Bloomington, IN 47403
www.authorhouse.com
Phone: 1-800-839-8640

First published by AuthorHouse 9/30/2011

ISBN: 978-1-4567-5698-7 (e)
ISBN: 978-1-4567-5699-4 (sc)

Printed in the United States of America

*I was inspired to write this book because of a special love
I loss so many years ago*

*WRITTEN BY
AVIS R. WATERS*

I sincerely, hope this book is able to help someone who is struggling within, seeking justice.

To bring, hope to those in despair.

To guide, those who are loss in the world, seeking for a place to belong.

And peace, to those who can not find their way out of darkness.

Developing, confident in yourselves, incentive to strive for what you believe in, and assertiveness to conquer any challenge that is put before you.

Always, pray and ask for serenity to except the things you cannot change and courage to change the things you can.

Family prayer is very important always, pray with your children daily, teach them of the marvelous Works of their creator, which is God.

For me, writing this book was the most therapeutic, therapy I needed to be set free.

CHAPTER

ONE

When I recall my childhood I think of the simple life and times. Living with my grandmother was wonderful. There was constantly something going on like barbecues, picnics, parties, Easter, and all the excitement of the night lights. Indeed, I really enjoyed sitting on my grandmothers front porch located on the main street of Superior Avenue which was busy all night long. However, my good times would shortly be coming to an end. You see, my mother and father purchased a house. Soon after my mom and dad purchased the house we moved in. After, living their I saw people walking in the night. However, when I told my mother and my father they told me that they were ghost. Also, my mom and dad told me that they wouldn't bother me so Just go to bed and pretend they are not there.

However, I was still afraid of them, they were scary, and spooky. In fact, I was afraid to go to bed at night. Another thing I started to notice was at night I would see pictures and movies while sleeping, when I told my mother and father about them they told me that they were dreams ironically, my dreams would come true. Every night, I would dream of black murky water in which I was drowning. Every night, I would have some kind of nightmare and then when I wake up from the nightmares and dreams there were the ghosts. As a child I did not know that dreams had meaning. All, I knew was every time I would go to sleep I would see pictures and movies in my sleep which would come true on a daily basis. Life was good for a few years. I, enjoyed traveling to Philadelphia for summer vacations especially seeing my cousins. There was always a big cookout and, we could drink all of the sodas we wanted.

Unfortunately, some years later my father lost his job. Our family was under financial stress. My parents, was constantly arguing each day was horrible. When, my mother would get angry at my father she would call her brothers over to beat up my dad. As soon, as my uncles would arrive usually, two of them would wrestle my father upstairs to the bathroom and jump on him. When, my uncles were done beating up my dad he would have busted lips, black eyes, and his face and hands would be swollen. Therefore, the continued fights and arguments was taking a toll on my father. As a result, my father turned to alcohol drinking every day. This, enhanced the domestic violence. Every, time there was an argument leading to a fight my mother would faithfully call her brothers on my dad. And, if my mother couldn't find her brothers she would call the police and make up a BIG lie about my father or what he supposedly had done to her.

Unfortunately, my grandfather was also an alcoholic in fact, he was a happy drunk who would pass out after he would eat a plate of food and drink a jug of booze. Nevertheless, I did not want to see my father go down the same path. Visits, from my grandfather was fun although, my parents were constantly arguing and fighting when my grandfather would visit somehow, he would make things better. Everything, my grandfather ate he would grow or kill it. My grandfather, would kill rabbits, squirrels, raccoons, and then he would drop them into a large pot of boiling water and beer after that he would skin them and clean them. After, the meat was done he would make up some kind of stew with gravy and rice for his dinner. After all, my grandfather expected us to eat it too. The only one that would eat my grandfathers stew and rice was my father. Of course, both of them were drunk.

My grandfather, also had stinky feet. No one wanted my grandfather to remove his shoes or socks. One thing that really puzzled me about my father and my grandfather was their skin color. My grandfather, looks like a white man but, his complexion was a little reddish, and his hair was brownish red and straight. This, was something I did not understand. As a child I wasn't allowed to ask many questions. I was told children should be seen and not heard. Trust me, they meant it in fact, I got a lot of spankings all the time.

Therefore, one day I was outside in the backyard with my grandfather one evening. I could not take the confusion anymore so, I asked my grandfather why, was his skin color different from my fathers also myself and everyone else in my family. My grandfather started to laugh at me then, he explained to me that his mother who was my great-grandmother was born full blooded Cherokee Indian. Also, I asked my grandfather about his father my great grandfather I wondered, if he also was Cherokee Indian. My grandfather said no my father is not Cherokee Indian he is a Negro. Now, I wondered again what is a Negro. At that time my grandfather explained to me that when your skin color is dark, and your hair is an afro, this makes you a Negro. During, this era people were wearing afros. Also, my grandfather said that Negros sometimes can be light skinned to. Now, I am more confused than ever before besides, I wanted to ask more questions but, I left it along. Nevertheless, my grandfather was a handsome man. I have always been attracted to men that favors my grandfather.

All through, I still did not understand why my father was so dark and my grandfather was so light so I decided to ask him one more question, how does his mother look and my grandfather replied, she is of African and Jamaican descent. In fact, a few years later my father's mother and sister came to visit and my grandmother was a dark complexion just like my father, I still find all of this confusing but maybe one day I will understand it. While, my aunt and grandmother was visiting my parents were trying to not let them know about our financial situation or the status in which their marriage was in. Therefore, my father was still looking for employment and to make our financial situation worse my mother found out she was pregnant for the third time. However, my father found a job working at a big fancy restaurant in fact, my dad brought home lots of good stuff to eat, my dad also gave the neighbors scraps for their dogs. Besides, my father and our next door neighbor were good friends Mr. Jake made homemade wine and he would often give my father a bottle. Mr. Jake, also had a grapevine in his backyard and he would give us fresh grapes.

However, at this time my mother was showing with the pregnancy, my dad was doing better with his drinking and was spending a lot of time with his father after church on Sundays we will go over to visit him there was always something my grandfather had cooked up. Springtime, was here and my brothers birthday was in May every year he would have a nice birthday party with friends, cousins, music, barbecue hamburges, hotdogs, and fun. My, birthday was at the end of the summer late August but I never had a birthday party if it wasn't for my godmother I'd probably would not have had a cake, she would bake me a cake for my birthday every year. But, I still don't understand to this day why, I never had a birthday party with friends, cousins, and fun.

Now, it is time to go back to school. In fact, returning

back to school was sad for me, I never got new clothes unless I saved eagle stamps and redeem them. Sometimes it would take a whole year to save up two books of eagle stamps. Each book of eagle stamps was three dollars however, back then things were cheap. Also new shoes. All my clothes were from the goodwill and they were smelly, and the rest of them were hand-me-downs from my cousins, I had a lot of cousins my mother had four brothers so therefore, there was a lot of hand-me-downs. However, my brother always got a lot of new clothes and shoes for school, and you should have seen the smile and the dance he would do when he was happy, he was always happy to get new clothes and shoes. Better yet, I had some other issues to deal with not only did I not like going to school in hand-me-down clothes or having a pack of dogs waiting for me outside every morning. I did not know why the dogs were waiting for me every morning, but I soon found out it was the bacon grease that I used every morning for lotion. However, my brother and I did not get alone, we had daily fights nor would my brother help me when a kid would pick fights with me, also we grew up in a all white neighborhood and I was called Nigger and darkie every day. Sometimes, I wish my brother would wait or walk to and from school with me, you see we went to school in the early 60's.

CHAPTER TWO

B y, this time my baby brother had arrived and he was cute as ever. However, I did not know I would be the one doing most of the work for the baby. My mother had me rinsing out diapers with BM in them in the toilet. In fact, I was only 8 years old and my mother had me hanging clothes out on the clothes line outside, using the washing machine, folding clothes and cleaning the house. However, my brother Howard started taking music lessons playing the violin. Better yet, all my brother had to do was his homework, practice his music, and boy did he sound terrible, and play outside. However, the only time I could play outside was when all the laundry was done, homework, dishes, and helping with my baby brother it was time for bed time. This was my every day life. If it wasn't for school I would not have seen other children unless I was looking out of the window.

By the time my baby brother Alex was three years old he started beating every thing he could get his hands on. Not only was Alex my baby brother he was also my only companion. Fortunately, the summer was here, school was out and our family was going on a vacation to Philadelphia. I was so excited to be going away for the summer after all, I would have a whole week and a half of not doing homework or taking care of my baby brother. Nevertheless, when my family and I arrived in Philadelphia nothing had changed I still had to care for, and look after my baby brother Alex. One night my girl cousins were going to hang out and have a sleepover at aunt Ethel's house however, my mother said I could not stay over. My mother said you are going to stay with me and your father so that you can keep an eye on Alex. Of course, I begged my mother to let me stay over my aunt's house with my cousins. My mom still said no your father and I have plans. Nevertheless, my aunt stepped in and said come on let her stay with the other girls tonight. As a result, my aunt talked my mother into letting me stay but, she wasn't happy about it.

Unfortunately, to make a long story short my parents got drunk and was not watching my brother. Alex wandered outside that night and was hit by a 10 speed bike. The person riding the bike was going so fast that my brother was hit so hard that from the extreme trauma he suffered a fractured skull. Alex was chewing gum and, the gum was in the back of his throat which cut off the oxygen supply to his brain. Therefore, my mother and I had to stay in Philadelphia while Alex was in the hospital. My father and my older brother Howard went back home to Cleveland. Indeed, my father had to return back to work and of course, my mother blamed me for my brothers accident. In fact, this is something she repeatedly scolded me about. My situation at home became worse. Finally, Alex was released from the children's hospital in Philadelphia. I was so happy to see my baby brother but, I did not expect to see his head wrapped up like a mummy as soon as I saw him I began to cry also, I was afraid to touch him.

Finally, my mother, baby brother, and myself could finally go home. After all, I was going to miss playing with my cousins, and eating good food every day fried chicken, pork chops, hamburgers and French fries, pancakes for breakfast. We caught the Greyhound bus back to Cleveland my father and brother was their to pick us up from the bus station. However, returning home was a night mare with constant visits to the hospital for Alex, constant arguments between my parents, also nothing had changed for me in fact, I had more responsibilities at home than before but, of course, Howard only had home work also, practice his instrument, by now, Howard, started to play the saxophone and after music lessons he would go outside to play. What a life. After, paying bills, medical attention for Alex, and expensive music lessons for Howard there was never enough money. unfortunately, after I came home from Philadelphia my older brother Howard started molesting me in fact, he would tell me if you tell I will choke you in your sleep and he would and lie about it and my mother would believe him, you see she ran the house my father was afraid to voice his opinion due to the fact, that my mother would call her brothers over to jump on my dad.

By now, I started my period. In fact, I was in a lot of pain when I was on it, but no one cared about me or any conditions I had to deal with, you see I was Cinderella without the wicked stepsister's. Finally, I was graduating from the six grade and I was surprised when my mother bought me a white blouse and a navy blue skirt for graduation. Brand-new. After, I came home from graduation nothing was different I had all my chores waiting for me and after caring for my younger brother it was bedtime. Summer vacation was horrible and I hated to be left alone with my older brother because, he would try to molest me, I had to fight with all my might with my brother daily. By now, my mother had started working in the evening and of course, I became a nanny for my younger brother Alex. Unfortunately, my parents marriage was over, and to make matters worse my parents received a phone call stating that my grandfather had collapsed on the streets and was in intensive care fighting for his life. However, my grandfather passed away at 55 years of age with cirrhosis of the liver. All, I could hear my mother say is when it rains it pours as if, we needed something else to go wrong. This, was the first funeral I had ever attended, it was very sad in fact, I had never seen so much food on one table in all my life people were constantly bringing all kinds of food over.

Unfortunately, my father had started back drinking alcohol on a daily basis and fighting with my mother constantly of course, she would call her brothers over as usual to beat up my dad but, this time they put my father out of our house. Where was he going to live I was worried about him all the time also, Alex was constantly asking for him as well. My mother, filed for divorce in fact, I jumped out of the pot into the frying pan because, I thought I had it bad but my life became worse. After, my parents divorce my mother started partying all the time every night there were strangers at the house playing music and drinking most of the night. Nevertheless, still playing the role of Cinderella cooking, laundry, cleaning, and taking care of Alex.

CHAPTER THREE

Returning, back-to-school was not easy, this year I started attending junior high and I did not know anyone. There were so many kids I had never seen before in fact, I was very nervous every day. Most of the girls were bullies and ran in packs. However I was a loner, I had no friends at this new school, my clothes were hand-me-downs and the majority of the girls had clothes that were in style. Every day, someone would point me out laughing at my clothes. After school, when I hand sometime I would try on clothes and remake them over to look like the styles the girls were wearing although, I had never had a sewing lesson I knew what to do. By now, my mother was still having a lot of parties at home sometimes my mother would not come home for days she would call and give me instructions on what to do about dinner, or Alex ect. Unfortunately, Howard and myself were still having daily arguments and fights he would put me in head locks, put my arm behind my back and hold it up to my head until I could not take the pain anymore but, the worst thing was when he put his weights at the top of the stairs, when I came out to my bedroom and started to go down the stairs I tripped over the weights. At that time I fell down a whole flight of stairs. The fights were becoming very dangerous because, there was no one to stop them. Every day, I was so consumed with daily survival also, I lived in fear every day of my life. When my mother would return home Howard would always lie and tell my mother I started the fights and that I was on the phone and not doing my work at home of course, she would believe everything he said so I was back in trouble again for nothing.

By this time I was 13 years old with a body like a pop bottle in fact, I have started getting a lot of attention from boys. My mother nevertheless, experiencing the single life were dating the wrong kind of men some of the men she was dating was married because their wives would come over our house knocking on the door and when I answered the door they would say where is the fat bitch that's fucking with my husband, tell her that when I see her I'm going to kick her fat ass. The other men my mother was dating was alcoholics, bums, and drug addicts I know this because I used to sneak downstairs in the middle of the night and, I saw them smoking something with a weird smell. Some of her male friends would say inappropriate comments to me, and their only focus was to exploit myself by touching me unfortunately, when I told my mother about her friends making inappropriate comments to me and touching me, my mother immediately became verbally abusive towards me, calling me a liar stating that no one wants you.

At this time, there were other problems, our house was in bad shape, our yard needed grooming, and one day there was a funny smell in the house, my mother called the gas company out to check the furnace. Unfortunately, the furnace had a carbon monoxide leak and the furnace blew up while the gas man was doing an inspection. Thank God, there was no serious injury to the gas man in fact, he alerted my mother to get the carbon monoxide leak repaired as soon as possible. We barely had enough money to pay the bills and my mother was spending a lot of money partying and of course, she would never take Howard out of his expensive music school. By now, my father became a chronic alcoholic he lost his job so there was no child support for us. Therefore, the furnace repair was put on the back burner.

My relationship with my mother became worse. I was punished for anything and everything which I found confusing. I tried not to do anything wrong. After all, I was already doing all the housework, caring for my younger brother Alex continued daily fight with my older brother Howard in fact, the only time my mother would talk to me was to give orders on what to do, or nasty verbal comments. As a result, I started to become very depressed each day my depression became worse however, I do not want to live life anymore each day I would fight the desire. As a result, I took a lot of my mothers pills that was in the medicine cabinet. My mother was very angry at me when I ended up in emergency. She found me collapsed on the living room floor. When I returned home that night nothing had changed their were still parties every night. My punishment became more severe now after all my chores I was locked in my room every evening.

Alex, was eventually diagnosed by his physician with deterioration of the brain and schizophrenia. With constant changes occurring with Alex my mother would turn to food she already had a weight problem in fact, she was extremely obese and, a compulsive eater. Finally, things did get better for me at school. I met a friend. Her name is Asia. Now, I have someone to walk to and from classes with also to eat lunch with we were in mostly the same classes. One day, after school my new friend Asia's brother came to pick her up from school and she introduced me to her brother Marvin. However, Marvin was the most handsome boy I ever saw in my life. In fact, my friend Asia and her brother were native Indian but was raised in a black neighborhood. The next day in school Asia told me that her brother thought I was beautiful and wanted to walk me home after school after all, this was the best thing that ever happened to me. Therefore, every day after school he would wait for me however, I was afraid to let Marvin walk me home, I was afraid of what my mother or brother would do if they saw him with me so I would only let him walk me to the corner of my street. Marvin, was not like any other boy I ever met, he was so kind, and sweet, he was also very funny he would make me laugh all the time.

I would go home and think about Marvin all the time but, I had to sneak in and call him on the phone if my brother found out I was on the phone he would tell my mother and I would be in even more trouble than I am already, in fact, I did not have to do anything wrong to get in trouble, all my brother has to do is tell my mother a lie about me and I would be beaten and punished. One day, while Marvin was walking me home from school he insisted in walking me to my door I told him I don't think that would be a good idea Marvin said what can happen all I am doing is walking with you we are not doing anything wrong. However, Marvin did not know my family history. In spite, of my reservations I let Marvin walk me to my door this was a big mistake usually my mother wasn't home after school but this day she was home and on the porch, and she saw Marvin this handsome, beautiful Indian boy of course, she yelled at me called me names and embarrassed me in front of Marvin better yet, my mother yelled at Marvin as well and told him to not ever come over here again.

Therefore, Marvin answered okay turned and walked away as I walked up to the porch my mother told me, I will make it so that he will never want you again. Although, I did not understand what she meant by that however, I would soon find out. The next day after school Marvin was there to walk me home as usual. I apologized to him for what happened. Now, you see why I did not want you to walk me home also Marvin was concerned about why I could not call him on the phone I tried to explain to him about my life of course, he did not understand. One day, I overheard my mother talking on the phone she said that if she did not get the furnace repaired our house would be condemned. I was praying every day that our furnace would be replaced. However, when I came home from school this particular day I was very unhappy to find the bully that would always spit on me and call me names in my living room talking to my mother. Unfortunately, the next day when I came home from school again Dennis the bully was at my house. My older brother was at his music lesson, and my younger brother was in the backyard playing. Therefore, I asked Dennis angrily, why are you here and he replied your mother wants me to paint the inside of your house.

CHAPTER FOUR

I was so confused, we need a new furnace not our house painted. Also, there was no paint or any painting supplies. The site of Dennis made me sick to my stomach I could not stand him and now he is an my house alone with me every evening my mother worked second shift. In fact, Dennis would always pick on me however, a few days later he started touching me inappropriately. I begged him to leave me alone, I did not like him at all he had tormented me every day on my way home from school and now he is in my house every day after school with me alone. Unfortunately, one day when I arrived home from school Dennis started to touch me inappropriately I begged please, please leave me alone but he wouldn't therefore, I started to run up the stairs trying to get to my bedroom however, Dennis chased me when he caught me, he began to tear my pants off me he was very aggressive and rough then he brutally raped me on the stairs when he finished, my vaginal area was wet I went into the bathroom to wash myself that night when my mother came home I told her what Dennis had done to me I wasn't surprised to hear her say you are a liar Dennis did not rape you and the next day he continued to come over and I was constantly left alone in the house with him.

When, I went to school I did not tell anyone what happened to me not even Asia. I was so embarrassed however, she could tell something was wrong with me. After, school her brother was waiting to walk me home however, Marvin wanted to talk. He started asking me a lot of questions about Dennis also, he wanted to know why he couldn't come over but Dennis could I tried to explain to him that my mother hired Dennis to paint our house on the inside. However, Dennis was merely a distraction, my mother knew my brother was molesting me therefore, she would leave Dennis at home with me. You see she did not want me to become pregnant by my brother. How would she explain this to her family members and, tarnish her spotless reputation. Every day, Marvin would walk down my street in the evening every day and he did not see anyone painting. Unfortunately, a month later my period did not come Dennis, was still coming over every day raping me and there was no one I could go to for help. Nevertheless, my mother continue to have wild parties. However, every night I wanted to tell my mother about my period but, I was afraid. Unfortunately, over time I noticed changes to my body and my breasts were always sore also, I was craving different kinds of food. One night, I was in my room with the door shut and I started to squeeze my breasts milk was in them this one particular night I was in my room and I started squeezing my breasts however, my brother busted in my room at the same time I was squeezing my breast he saw the milk coming out in fact, he could not wait for my mother to come home to tell her.

Upon, my mother's arrival home my brother told her what he saw my mother immediately assumed that I was pregnant by Marvin. However, I told her that I was not pregnant by Marvin she then asked, who is it and I replied it's Dennis I told you that he raped me. Besides after my mother found out about Marvin I was not allowed for him to walk me home anymore also, my mother notified the school to let her know if I had cut school in fact, I was never able to be alone with Marvin therefore, I knew that it was between Dennis or my brother Howard. Nevertheless, my mother scheduled a doctor's appointment for me and the pregnancy test was positive at this time I was still going to school and in spite of everything Marvin would still walk me to the corner of my street. Unfortunately, the walks, the fun, and the laughter was gone from me and from Marvin eventually I had to tell Marvin what happened to me and that I was pregnant, also, I would be transferring to another school. Finally, Dennis told my mother that he had been having sex with me but of course, my mother blamed everything on me and Dennis got away scot- free with everything he had done to me instead, I was the one who was verbally abused every day while I was pregnant.

Nevertheless, nothing had changed at home. At this time, I was about five months pregnant, and it was Christmas time. On Christmas Eve my mother and her friends was doing their usual partying as a result, someone turned off the furnace after all, they were hot from drinking and dancing half the night. However, the next morning the house was extremely cold inside. Therefore, Howard was the one who would light the furnace, not thinking about the carbon monoxide leak Howard went downstairs in the basement and lit the furnace unfortunately, the furnace blew up on him causing third degree burns to his hands, and face the only reason his chest did not get burned because the house was so cold inside Howard put on his winter coat. This ordeal really sobered mom and her friends up in fact, she had to get herself together to take Howard to the emergency room. Howard, was in the hospital for a couple months, a couple of months of peace for me and even though he was always mistreating me I still felt sorry for him and I prayed for him daily.

At Lease, I could sneak and call Marvin sometimes, I shared with him how my Christmas was. When, I told him about my brother he was very sorry for him after all, I couldn't see Marvin at school anymore however, Marvin was heartbroken when I transferred to a school for pregnant teenagers. As a result, Marvin quit school and joined the military in fact, he told me that he had a job and if I needed anything he would be happy to help me. Marvin was the only person who ever tried to help me but, he was defenseless against the evil forces of my mother and brother who were bred evil. Marvin could never have understood what was going on in my house. Even the house was evil, there were rats, ghost, and spiders. Every day, I would pray even though things never changed. By now, my brother, Howard, was out of the hospital, his return home was a nightmare. Not only was Howard up to his same old tricks, I was also a nurse maid for Howard however, this did not stop him from getting me in trouble and telling everything I do to my mother. One day, I called Marvin on the phone as a result, my brother told my mother, and my mother told Dennis therefore, Dennis jumped on me and beat me up while I was pregnant while my mother and my brother just watched like it was a TV show.

After, Dennis finished beating me up I went up to my room and everyone went on with their evening as if nothing had happened however, no one showed any concern for me. Now, I can't even talk to Marvin on the phone anymore I missed him so much if he only knew that my life went from bad to worse. Unfortunately, after the furnace blew up on my brother the city condemned our house and we had to move and to make matters worse we moved into the projects. At this time, the focus was on my pregnancy. Therefore, my mother and Dennis told Dennis mother about the pregnancy of course, his mother was furious about just finding out about my pregnancy. However, my mother and Dennis never included me in any of their conversations. One day, my mother and Dennis was talking and I over heard my mother tell Dennis you have to marry her, the next day I ran away from home and I called my father to come and pick me up, and he did he also called my mother to come and get me I was so hurt I wanted to live with my father.

After, returning back home, I was punished severely in fact, I couldn't read the letters that Marvin would send me or, be able to talk to him ever again even Marvin's sister tried contacting me but of course, I wasn't able to talk to her either. Unfortunately, the abuse started to take a different course. You see, my mother started using other people to inflict it. After all, Dennis and my mother were constantly discussing my pregnancy and the two of them arranged a shot gun wedding between Dennis and myself. Dennis mother was strongly against it. I was happy with his mother's decision I still don't understand how my mother talked Dennis into marrying me, I was a child. After, a few weeks passed I would overhear my mother and Dennis planning the marriage. Although, Dennis did not listen to the concerns that his mother had about him getting married. Dennis was 19 or 20 years old and, was able to make its own decisions. Besides I had no say about anything also, I was not included in any planning or conversations concerning this matter.

Better yet, the biggest most important factor is that Dennis is a stranger that beats me that controls my life, someone I despise and hate and my mother knew how I felt. Every day, I would come home from school upset also, I expressed daily to my mother how I felt. One morning, my mother woke me up very early. At the foot of my bed was a lavender dress and some brown patent leather dress shoes. I was told to get dressed after my bath so I did what I was told. Dennis arrived about an hour later. Unfortunately, I knew what was going on this was the day I regretted the day I was going to get married. In fact, my mother and Dennis had already applied for the marriage license you see, I was a minor so my mother had to sign for me to get married also, she made up some kind of story about me being a wild out of control teenager. How could I be a out of control teenager when I was not allow to go anywhere or have any friends. The only places I was allowed to go was to school and, to the store. However, this was her reason for marrying me off. As long as her reputation was spotless that's all that mattered. She did not want anyone to know about all the evil, devious, abusive things that she was doing to me.

Unfortunately, we were married downtown at the courthouse. After we were married I went back home change my clothes and stayed in my room that night and every night after that I was forced to have sex with Dennis while my mother listened. There were constant beatings from Dennis while my mother watched also, if Dennis could not find anything to beat me up about my mother would tell him any lie she could think of to make him beat me. My older brother, Howard was about to graduate from high school. Nevertheless, the brutal beatings from Dennis continued throughout my whole pregnancy. Finally, it was time for the baby to arrive in fact, I was in labor for three days when the baby was born I was so relieved not to be pregnant anymore. The apperance of my body was horrible, sagging skin, and stretch marks everywhere it, was just a nightmare. I would just stand in the mirror and look at myself crying. However, I had never felt this kind of pain before, the pain was constant and I was sick the whole time I was in labor throwing up with every contraction. To make matters worse my mother stood over my bed chanting some kind of voodoo words.

CHAPTER

FIVE

Howered, the baby was healthy but she looked white. Dennis and myself were dark skinned so of course, everyone started denying the baby stating that Dennis was not the father but, the baby was his daughter I guess, the baby had taken after my grandfather who was part Indian and Black. The baby was so beautiful, and so perfect all I could do was thank God that the baby was not hurt during all the beatings while I was pregnant. Nevertheless, I was very depressed, unhappy and still being abused and raped by the stranger who was my husband daily while my mother watched and listened and after, all was said and done I still had my baby to take care of. Dennis, was very controlling in fact, I was not allowed to leave the apartment, talk on the phone, or have any friends, I was told what to eat and how to eat also, Dennis would put me on diets whenever he felt I had gained a few pounds. When, Dennis would leave for work he would lock my clothes and shoes in the closet. One day, my friend from school came over and I let her in we were having fun talking, and listening to music when Dennis came home from work he was furious and demanded my friend to leave as she started to walk down the stairs he kicked her and pushed her down the stairs he then jumped on me and I cried out to my mother please, please help me and she replied this is your husband, I cannot help you I then cried out to my mother and I said how come you will never help me when Dennis is beating me, why do you watch him do it, you are suppose to be my mother someone who is suppose to care about me and protect me and she replied again this is your husband and I cannot help you.

A week later, after being brutally beaten by Dennis again I was fed up there for, I went into the kitchen got a knife out of the drawer ran towards Dennis with all my might and I cut his throat as a result, my mother went ballistic and started jumping on me for cutting Dennis in fact, she rushed him to emergency, then called Dennis mother and sister and told them what happened therefore, the both of them came over to my mothers apartment to jump on me as well. After, my mother rushed Dennis to the hospital I locked the door when Dennis mother and sister came and started knocking and beating on the door I would not let them in after beating on the door for over 30 minutes or more they finally left. As a result, I packed my babies things I walked over to my friend Jennifer's house she was one of my friends from school when I arrived at her house I begged her mother to let me and my baby stay for the night I told her what had happened and you could see that I have been beaten up my face was swollen, my eyes and lips were busted and swollen about time I arrived at my friends I was very fatigue and exhausted. I was lucky that my friends mother let me stay considering she had eight kids of her own and was on public assistance.

Therefore, the next day Jennifer's mother told me I could stay but, I would have to go downtown and apply for welfare, so that I would have some kind of income for my baby and myself so I did. Indeed, I applied and was accepted for welfare benefits and medical for my daughter and myself however, I was going to receive a check and food stamps as well. Unfortunately, my mother and Dennis were out looking for me and the baby one day there was a knock at my friends door it was them they had came to to take me back home I told them my friends mom said that I could live with them. Immediately, my mother asked who was going to take care of us financially I proudly told her that I was approved to receive welfare benefits so I have income for myself and my daughter. By now, my mother was speechless for a moment and then she asked my friends mother are you sure you can handle this and she stated yes she knew what I was going through at home.

Therefore, I was afraid to go home with my mother and Dennis I had no one to protect me there, all I could do was call on God's mercy and his serenity and encourage to go on every day living in a nightmare However, I was trying to change my life in fact, I wanted to go back to school. Better yet, my friends mom said she would watch my baby while I was attending school. Nevertheless, my mother and Dennis was up to no good plotting against me trying to figure out a way to get me to come back home you see, neither Dennis nor my mother would admit to the accusations against them after all neither of them wanted anyone to know of the horrible things that was going on at their apartment. Although, I wasn't really happy living there but at least I wasn't getting beat up and raped by the stranger my mother married me off to. A week later, I received a phone call from my mother she said, I'm sorry for all the things I did to you and I want to be a mother to you. My mother then stated, you are young and need to enjoy your life, have some fun. My mother also said I don't mind babysitting the baby. However, I found this to be strange my mother, has never offered to watch my baby for me.

I was ecstatic, I couldn't believe what I was hearing after all, this was something I had been praying for every day. Therefore, I packed the babies things, went over to my mother's with my baby however, my mother was very pleasant to me I had never seen her so pleasant, and nice to me before. Therefore, I kissed my baby and I thanked my mother repeatedly I then told my mother that I would be calling later and that I would be over tomorrow evening to pick up the baby my mother replied no problem don't worry about nothing and have a good time with your friends. Sunday, I called my mother and I told her that I was on my way to pick up the baby my mother said okay I will have her ready when you get here. When, I arrived my mother would not answer the door so I continued to knock on the door still no answer.

At this time, I started to call out are you in there please let me in still no answer I then started knocking on the kitchen window also, looking trying to see what was going on. I did not know, my mother was boiling a pot of water on the stove also she had called the police on me and before the police arrived my mother opened the kitchen window at this time I was standing in front of the window trying to see what was going on. At this time, my mother picked up the pot of boiling water and threw the boiling water on me in fact, my mother was so anxious to throw the boiling water on me that she did not praise God get the water hot enough to scald my skin at this time I went crazy, I was soaking wet and the water was hot and somehow I managed to break the kitchen window. By this time, the police had arrived my mother finally opened the door and started shouting get her, she is no good, she is a tramp, she run's the streets looking for Tom, Dick, and Harry. My mother, also told the police that I had left my daughter with her and that I never came back for weeks to pick her up after repeated phone calls to me. At this time, the police noticed blood dripping from my right hand, I did not know that I had cut my baby finger actually, my finger was cut halfway off at this time the police rushed to me to emergency to have my finger sewed back on. After, the doctor had sewed my finger back to my hand

I was discharged from the hospital. The police told me not to go back to my mothers apartment today. In fact, the police told me to wait and let things die down so I went back to my friend Jennifer's house.

The following Monday my mother and Dennis went downtown to the welfare office and told them that I was in the streets, my mother also stated that she had care of my daughter for many months. Unfortunately, my only means of support was cut off immediately. Therefore, Jennifers mother told me I could not stay there anymore. As a result, I was forced to go back to my mothers house. Instead, my mother applied for my benefit at the welfare office now, my mother is receiving my check and food stamps she would not give me anything, not even a $.50 food stamp to buy a candy bar. However, my mother saved up all the checks and bought herself and my brother a car, every month Howard would drive down from college and my mother and Howard would go grocery shopping then Howard would load up his car with food, and personal hygiene items and of course, Howard, was given half of the check. Although, Dennis was working I was not given any money from him either, he knew I would run away. He just made sure that I had personal hygiene items and food etc. however, I spent most of my days at my sewing machine, sometimes I would sew from morning to night only taking out time to prepare meals, and care for my daughter. As a result, some of Dennis friends would ask me to sew for them after all, Dennis did not mind me sewing for his friends this made him look important.

At this time, I started to notice that the relationship

Avis R. Waters

between my mother and Dennis was not normal. In fact, they were not acting as son-n-law or mother-in-law. Better yet, they did everything together every day the two of them would go shopping, out to dinner on a regular basis sometimes after I had gone to bed Dennis would stay up for hours with my mother watching TV or sometimes sitting on the porch. By now, I realized that my mother was in love with Dennis in fact, she saw me as a threat. Each day of my life was filled with hatred, jealousy, and verbal and physical abuse. One day, Dennis arrived home from work and stated that his coworker had an apartment for rent. Of course, Dennis and my mother discussed everything without me however, I was hoping that Dennis would rent the apartment. Nevertheless, a few days later, I overheard Dennis telling my mother that he had put down a deposit for the apartment. After all, I was so happy to be moving from my mother. Each day, I prayed that things would be different for me after we move. Unfortunately, nothing changed, my mother would visit daily, all most, every night they would go out together while my daughter and myself stayed home and watched TV, which wasn't bad at all I enjoyed spending time with my daughter and being at home alone however, sometimes when Dennis would return home he would, start verbally and physically abusing me.

One day, I was thinking about Dennis and my mothers relationship and I realized why my mother wanted me to marry Dennis, she wanted to keep Dennis close to her. Yet, knowing that Dennis was sleeping with me at night drove her to be insanely jealous. As a result, the abuse I suffered from my mother took a different direction however, my mother used other people to inflict subtle unpleasant situations when I would come around family members in fact, there was always a big embarrassing moment staged involving myself whenever I attended a family party, or barbecue there was nowhere I could go and have a good time. Eventually, everything was starting to take a toll on me, there was no one to talk to, nowhere to turn, I had no friends also Dennis relationship with our daughter was always negative and brutal as if he regretted her existence, which he was totally responsible for Besides, my daughter wasn't happy unfortunately, she saw her father constantly verbally and physically abusing me in fact, it was so sad when my daughter would beg her father to stop beating me and, she was only three years old.

CHAPTER SIX

After being in a constant state of extreme depression each day was a constant struggle. My loss of appetite was becoming worse in fact, I have lost three pants sizes in weeks also I suffered with fatigue and dizziness, my menstrual period was irregular which results in Pre and post menstrual syndrome. After, great observation of my life I felt my daughter would be better off without myself and the miserable life in which we were living. In fact, I'd rather see my daughter happy with another family than to be brutally unhappy living with Dennis and myself. One day, I asked my neighbor to watch my daughter for a few hours well, this is what I told her after Dennis left for work. Eagerly, my neighbor agreed to look after my daughter beside, she knew what my living conditions consist of. Therefore, I went back to my apartment in a deep state of depression I just wanted to end it all, I just kept thinking there is no way out of this mess I have no life, I have no joy, there is no laughter, no fun, I have no friends, I can't even come and go as I please without getting jumped on.

Therefore, I went and found some rope in the closet then I went and got a chair out of the kitchen. I then stood on the chair and tied the rope to the vent over the bedroom door at this time I tied the rope around my neck and kicked the chair out from under me by now, I felt my skin on my neck busting open, I felt the pressure in my eyes as if my eyeballs were popping out indeed, I felt my life slowly slipping away then suddenly someone came through the door, it was Dennis to this day I don't know why Dennis did not go to work however, he saved my life immediately he ran into the kitchen and got a knife he then grabbed my legs and held me up to stop me from strangling and cut the rope down from the vent. After he got me down he carried me to the bed and laid me down he then asked me where our daughter was and I told him that she was with the neighbor next door. Therefore, Dennis went over to talk to her however, she agreed to look after our daughter the rest of the night. When Dennis returned back to the apartment he stayed in the living room the rest of the night.

As a result, the next day Dennis told me that he wasn't going to let my mother use him to hurt me anymore. Surprisingly, he apologized to me, he also stated that he was angry at himself for what he had did to his life and my life better yet, he felt trapped in this marriage and that his life was going nowhere. Therefore, a little over a week later Dennis enlisted into the Air Force two weeks before he was scheduled to leave Dennis stayed with my mother. Finally, he is going to let me go. As soon as I was free I immediately contacted Marvin however, my mother was right he did not want anything to do with me. Now I understand what she meant when she stated I will make it so that he will never want you again. If Marvin only knew how I had to fight every day for years just to see him. Also, all the beatings I endured because, I would call for him while sleeping. This would make Dennis so angry. He knew he would never have my heart. During, basic training Dennis began to send money to me. As soon, as I had enough money saved I filed for divorce. However, I did not know I was about to enter into another dilemma. After, Dennis had left for the military my mother went ballistic in fact, she tried in every way she could to destroy me after all, the sad thing was I couldn't even imagine the things that she was planning to hurt me with pre-meditated situations. Unfortunately, it was like I was on a battlefield I never knew when I was going to walk into one of her explosions. Nevertheless, I tried to stay away from my mother at all costs. I managed to return back to school in fact, my school assisted me in finding a job working at the VA hospital, my school also arranged childcare for my daughter, and paid for my public transportation.

By now, I was trying to regroup and find myself, striving each and every day to get my life together. Also, I stayed as far away from my mother as I could. Unfortunately, one day my mother showed up at my job caused a scene trying to get me fired. However, I don't know how she found out where I worked. Fortunately, I had been a good employee, never late, and had perfect attendance therefore, my job did not hold what my mother did against my employment in fact, everyone gave me a lot of support. Although, while all of this was going on I met Johnny. Johnny, was just discharged from the Vietnam war and was working at the VA hospital also. After, seeing me use public transportation to get home from work in the evenings Johnny offered me a ride home in his beautiful brand-new Candy Apple red sports car. Of course, I accepted the ride. Johnny became more like a hanging partner in fact, Johnny, my daughter, and myself was together a lot doing fun things. Finally, I was experiencing laughter and joy. As a result, Johnny and I were becoming very close which was against his parents approval. Even though, Johnny was 25 years old his parents had a huge influence over his life and his decisions. Nevertheless, I did not let his parents and there reservations stop me from seeing Johnny.

After, eight months of dating Johnny and I eloped and was married, his parents was not happy. Oh well, there was nothing they could do we were already married. Nevertheless, his family was not thrilled about Johnny moving out. After all, I was 19 years old, renting my own house which was fully furnished and carpeted. My house was beautiful there were plants hanging from the ceiling in beautiful macramé plant holders in which I hand made. Also, I was tailoring men's clothes and was making 5 to 6 hundred dollars a week. When, Johnny's parents and sister came over and saw my beautiful plaid furniture, earth tones shag carpet, color TV, stereo, and bedroom furniture for my daughters room and mine they were speechless they found it hard to believe that at my age I had all of this. Besides, I also made everything I wore for myself and my daughter we had beautiful clothes in fact, my hair was always in a beautiful style, also, I put colorful ribbons and bows in my daughters hair. After all, I had it going on, this messed up their heads.

In spite, of little ups and downs, verbal outbursts from his mother and sister we managed to be happy for four years. At this time, I found out I was pregnant. Therefore, my husband and myself decided to move into a bigger house of our own. Of course, this was against his parents approval again however, we continue looking. In fact, while out on our journey we found a beautiful baby mansion in the suburbs, in our price range. My husband was a honorably discharged Vietnam veteran with a G.I. loan. Of course, we went for it, we purchased our home. However, everyone pretended they were happy for us but in all reality they were mad as hell. Our new home was spectacular, there was a wood burning fireplace, a portrait of a big beautiful apple tree was painted from the ceiling to the floor in the living room, there were carpet all through the house even in the kitchen with a built-in stove and refrigerator, a breakfast den, a double porch, humongous front yard, three bedrooms, and a nursery for the baby.

Everyone was envious of our new home in fact, my mother was in shock to see I had accomplished something. My mother never wanted anything nice or good for me. Johnny's parents and sister kept a lot of confusion going on for example, one day my husband arrived home with his niece, a set of suitcases, and a long story. To make a long story short, my husband and his sister went behind my back and my husband legally adopted his niece without my knowledge. Johnny and his sister were constantly planning things without my knowledge. In fact, when his sister would enter our home she would not even speak or say hello. When his sister would come over to visit her daughter she would act as if my daughter and myself was not even in the house I was constantly disrespected and my husband allowed this to go on in fact, he supported his sister more than he supported me, my pregnancy, and his stepdaughter. Johnny never stood up for me as his wife the sad thing about this is I thought I knew my husband but, I found out I did not know him at all. To this day his sister has never thank me for caring for her daughter.

The day I went into labor his sorry sister or family did not come over to care or pick up her daughter the whole time I was in the hospital her daughter was at my house and she accompanied him to all the visits he made while I was in the hospital. As a result, the day I was discharged from the hospital with my new baby was horrible. I wanted my family, my husband, and my daughter to bond as a family with our new baby. Instead, my husband was too busy preparing dinner, helping with homework, and caring for his niece. However, Johnny did not pay very much attention to the baby better yet, he did not hold her or give her a bottle that was my job. Not one day after I came home with our new baby did his sister congratulated or thank me for caring for her child in fact, she never came over to our house during this time at all.

To make matters worse, I caught my husband cheating on me with the 17 year old girl next door. No wonder he was not interested in myself or the baby he was too busy trying to sneak outside to meet his girlfriend after caring for his niece, I wish he gave our new baby the same equal attention. Instead he was short tempered and distant. After finding out about his affair I packed some things for the baby and my daughter called my girlfriend Jennifer asked if myself and the children could stay with her for a few days. Jennifer asked what happened what's going on I told her I would explain everything to her later. Of course, you and the kids are always welcome so I moved out. That next day I contacted an attorney concerning this situation At this time I filed for a legal separation when I returned back to my house my husband had moved his sister, her boyfriend, her daughter was already living there and the girl next door had also moved in. Johnny, refused to give me any of my personal belongings also his sister had her refrigerator blocking the door so that I could not get any thing through the front door

Johnny and the girl next door moved in together. Some years later she became pregnant and delivered a baby boy. One day, upon his arrival home he caught her in the bed with another man. After all the ruckus was over she left him with the baby. To this day she has never returned. His son is now 15 years old. Unfortunately, his son do not know who his mother is or where she is.

All the time this was going on I was carrying my three month old daughter in her infant seat. After, entering the house I set the baby down in the hallway at this time, I demanded his sister to have the refrigerator moved away from the door, his sister replied no bitch this is my house now therefore, you are not getting anything out of here today so you should just take your baby and leave. This was her niece. From the first time I met my husbands sister she looked her nose down on me even throughout the marriage his sister would enter into my house without speaking to me or my other daughter. At this time, I was so angry about how his sister had been treating me in my house the whole time I was pregnant. As a result, everything had built up inside me before, I knew it I had punched his sister in the face then we started to fight. The next thing I know is my husband who promised to protect and honor me was helping his sister jump on me. Upon my observation, there was blood everywhere. In my anger, I had to thrown his sister through the glass door in the hallway. When my husband saw his sister bleeding he ran and grabbed a gun in fact, he owned many guns. As a result, he shot the gun into the ceiling while the baby was in her infant seat on the floor. Not once did he show any concern for his own baby.

I could not believe that he fired a gun in the vicinity of the baby. Buy now, my husband rushed his sister to the emergency room evidently, she had cut her arm on the glass from the hallway door. At this time, I left with my baby and immediately went to the police station. When I arrived there I gave the police a description of everything that happened also, I gave them my documents from my attorney. As a result, the police went out to the house saw the bullet hole in the ceiling. By this time Johnny and his sister had returned from the emergency room. At that time, the police arrested both Johnny and his sister for assault also, his sister was also charged with trespassing. My husband was charged with firing a gun in the present of an infant. Indeed, his parents were furious when they found out what was going on. Instead, of them being angry at my husband and his sister who were wrong, they were angry at me for going to the police. I have a right to stand up for what is legally mine which was my house. In fact, my husband should have been defending me not against me regardless of what happened. My heart would never forgive him for putting our baby in danger.

When it rains it pours. Guess who showed up at my door, my mother of course. At this time, I was staying with my friend Jennifer. Again, she found out where I was staying. When she arrived at my friend Jennifer's she told me again, I want to be a mother to you. Never once did she say she was sorry for any thing that happened before. All my mother said is I just want to help you. This was strange to me because, my mother has never offered to help me at all. For so long I have prayed to hear those words from my mother but I am sorry would you forgive me would have been more sufficient. During, this time I really need a lot of support while in court filing for divorce and dealing with constant court visits with the charges against my husband and his sister. I was going through a lot. Therefore, again I let my mother back into my life. A week later, my mother came to visit. During her visit, she started to tell me about a two family house that was for sale. Also, she asked me to go with her to look at the house. While riding to see the house my mother stated: since you are not with your husband anymore you and the children can have the downstairs and, I would take the upstairs if we get the house. Just think about it she said.

CHAPTER

SEVEN

Unfortunately, I did not listen to my friend or her advice. Jennifer, told me you Know that your mother and yourself have had a lot of negative issues. Therefore, I don't think this would be a good idea. Please think about this. Indeed, you and the children are welcome to stay here until you get on your feet. Of course, I went against Jennifer's advice. As a result, I told my mother that I would go in on the purchase of the house. At this time, I told my mother that I had $5000 saved up. Therefore, we proceeded in talking with the real estate agency. This real estate agency was shady in fact, they would make faulty document setting you up in a business. My mother set up a daycare center called Reeds Day Care Center. I used my real social security number and employment information. As a result, the financing was approved shortly after we moved into our house. What a big mistake I made first of all, my mother would throw her trash out of the window which resulted in rats and mice coming into the house. Therefore, I was the one who cleaned up the trash, cut the grass, groomed the yard, and took care of all the repairs concerning the house.

In fact, I did all the remodeling myself. In fact, I put up beautiful kitchen wallpaper also I wallpapered the bathroom, painted all of the other rooms, tiled the kitchen and bath room floors, carpeted living room floors, and also the bedrooms. I made sure that everything was nicely done. Even my mother was proud of all my work. Therefore, my mother invited a lot of our family members over to see our newly remodeled home. Finally, I felt that I had a family. Everyone was praising me, and telling me how great of a job I did in remodeling the house. For a while things were somewhat good. At this time, I purchased a pre-owned vehicle that was in mint condition. Ironically, a few weeks later I started to notice scratches on my car. So, I wondered who could be scratching my new car. Nevertheless, I approached my mother and asked her have you seen anyone in the backyard, my mother asked why, I told her someone was scratching my car. At this time my mother said its probably one of those no good niggers you were messing with.

This startled me, because at this time I was not involved with anyone in fact, I was recovering from my divorce. After, a week went by I noticed more and more scratches on my car. However, I told my next door neighbor what was going on concerning my car also, I asked my neighbor if I could camp out at her house so that I could watch my car. Also, I asked my next door neighbor if she would please keep an eye on my car. She replied, I would be glad to, she was a very sweet older lady who enjoyed the company of my children and myself. A week later, I told my mother that I was having some trouble with my car, and that the lady next door was going to give me a ride to work.

Little did she know, that myself and my neighbor was watching all of that day to see who was scratching my car. Unfortunately, as much as I hate to admit it, it was my mother. Each day, when my mother would leave for work she would look around to make sure no one was watching her, at that time she pulled a knife out of her purse then, started scratching my car. After that, my neighbor continue to watch my car for me. Nevertheless, my neighbor told me that every night when my mother would come home from work she would look around to make sure no one was watching at that time, she would scratch my car. Of course, I was heartbroken. I cannot believe my mother lied and deceived me again however, she was up to her same old tricks. As a result, when I confronted my mother she denied everything also, she began to yell at me saying you are a liar, you did not see me do anything. As much as I hate to admit it, my mother is an psychotic liar everything illegal, irrational, negative, and immoral I learned from my mother. After that, everything rapidly went downhill. There were constant arguments over the kids, and everything concerning the house. There were issues with the mail because, some of my mail came up missing in fact, there was always some kind of problem about this or that.

By now, I knew buying this house with my mother was a big mistake. I should have listened to my friend Jennifer who only had my best interests at heart. One evening, I received a call at work from my babysitter, she stated that my mother was knocking on my door or should I say banging on the door as described by my babysitter. When the babysitter answered the door my mother told her that my kids which is her grandchildren had broken her clothes dryer that was in the basement. At that time, I told my sitter to tell my mother that I would deal with it when I get off work and, I ended the call. About, 10 minutes later I received another call from my babysitter stating that my mother had a hatchet and, she had started to chop her way through the locked door. Also, there was a glass window which was broken out as well.

Finally, my mother succeeded in busting the door open you see my mother was extremely large women with a lot of strength. At that time, she preceded with a hatchet and chopped a huge dent in the side of my refrigerator which resulted in all of the fluids necessary for the refrigerator to freeze leaked out. Also, my mother started to destroy my living room furniture by cutting up the couch and, busting my lamps. When I returned home from work my whole house was a wreck. My mother destroyed everything I owned for no reason at all.

When my daughter was trying to stop my mother by pulling on her I was told my mother hit her in the face, my daughter is light skinned therefore, there were purple and red bruises all over her face. Better yet, the situation became worse that night my mother turned on all the water and let the water run all night destroying all of the flooring, she ripped off half of the wallpaper on the walls, she chopped big holes in the bedroom and living room walls, and poured bleach all over the carpet. As a result, the place was ruined. On the next morning ironically, there was a moving truck. How can you get a moving truck, and movers overnight to move you. This was meticulously plotted. After, my mother moved out she called all my uncles and family members told them that I had went into a rage and destroyed the house if things couldn't get worse all of my uncles came over to the house yelling up in my windows verbally abusing me calling me stupid bitch and other names I rather not say, you tore up your own house you dumb bitch.

Unfortunately, the house was so badly damaged I had to let it go black mold had started to grow from the water damage in the basement and, the damage to the house estimated around $50,000. However, since I used my real social security number and employment information my credit was ruined also I had to find somewhere else to move. After, that I did not see my mother again for over five years. Eventually, I found a place to stay. We moved in to our new place finally we were settled in, I had transferred the kids to their new school, and we were trying to put the past behind us. One day, while in the store I met a gentleman named Paul. Paul was very handsome with beautiful green eyes sometimes his eyes changed to Hazel. Paul, had a nice physique beautiful straight white teeth with a sexy walk. in fact, Paul paid a lot of attention to me he would call me several times a day when he would visit he was a gentleman also, he would bring me flowers but I'm quite sure he stole them out of somebody's yard however, he bought them for me nevertheless. Paul had an accident at work which resulted in him losing three of his fingers however, he was in pain all the time.

Paul, would invite my children and myself over to his apartment for dinner also, Paul would take us on trips every time he would take us on a trip he would stop and buy three tires and put them in the trunk of the car. We were off and on our way as we were driving on the turnpike I heard a loud sound one of the tires had a blowout so Paul pulled over like it was nothing, and changed the tire this went on a couple times while we were on our trip. By now, Paul and I, were becoming very close and my kids was starting to like him a little more. However, when Paul and I met it was in the summer, so I did not understand why he always wore long sleeves shirts when it was 90° outside. In fact, one night Paul removed his shirt and I noticed which look like needle sticks on his arms therefore, I ask Paul what it was and he told me that the phlebotomist always had a problem drawing his blood however, I wasn't in the medical field so I let it go.

CHAPTER EIGHT

Eventually, I started to notice some unusual behavior infact, I could not understand why every time Paul would use the bathroom there was a aerosol of blood on the bathroom wall. Therefore, I would wash the blood stains off the wall and they would appear again and again. The one thing I also did not understand was how he never noticed that blood was on the wall or that I washed the blood off. One day, before Paul came over for a visit I had taken a hammer and a nail and made a little peephole in the door. Upon, his arrival he went to use the bathroom so I started to peep through the hole in the door at this time, Paul pulled a little package out of his pocket and opened it he then removed his belt off his pants and wrapped it around his upper arm he then started to run the water, in his socks was a syringe which he used after he mixed the powder and the water together, and then he proceeded to inject it into his arm at that time I yelled out Paul I am looking at you through the door, Paul, became very nervous he hurried and cleaned up the stuff, came out of the bathroom sweating and shaking I've never been around drug addict but I've seen them on TV.

I immediately told him to leave my house and he did. As a result, I told Paul I could no longer date him or have him around my kids. Paul, started stalking me, and calling me repeatedly he would not leave me alone. One day, he came over to my house and was knocking on my door. I refused, to answer it. Perhaps, he thought I had another man in my house but I did not also I believe he had been drinking. At that time, Paul shot a gun through the window on the door. Thank God, Paul did not shoot any of us but it scared myself and the children very badly, and the children were shaken with fear. Immediately, I called the police and the whole SWAT team came, at that time when I told them his name I found out he had a rap sheet and had been in trouble numerous times trying to get drugs, he was addicted to heroin.

A few weeks later Paul contacted me and told me that he had enrolled in a methadone clinic, and was trying to get off the drugs, he apologized for what he did shooting the gun, also, he admitted to being high that night. Nevertheless, I did not want any else to do with him however, as a result, I ended up having to move again for the safety of myself and my children. Although, trying to find a place to stay was not easy in fact, I did not have a lot of money. As a result, I resigned from my job by doing this I could collect my retirement money which was about $7000. While, on my constant search to find a place to stay my children and myself checked into a weekly hotel for the welfare of our safety also, I put all my belongings in storage. Finally, three weeks later after constantly searching every day I found a nice place, in a nice area, with a wonderful school system, and the price was right. Surprisingly, the custodian who showed me the apartment did not ask for references. In fact, he rented the place to me and my children on the spot there for, I paid my rent five months in advance. Several months after moving in the custodian would always find a reason to knock on my door, so I asked him is this why you rented the place to me so you can constantly run up here for one thing or another. However, he replied yes, you are fine, at that time I told him, you are not going to be my landlord and my boyfriend to.

After, a year went by Joseph and I started to date. Soon after, I met his parents they were kind of weird nor did they talk very much to me, they would just look at me and my kids. Nevertheless, Joseph and I were spending a lot of time together. After, seven months of dating I became pregnant with my third child at this time, my youngest daughter was nine years old. Joseph, insisted that we get married, also, Joseph did not want our baby to be born out of wedlock. Therefore, I told him, I have to think about it after all, I had two children to consider. After, I thought about it I decided to marry him. After all, I rather be married than living with a man pregnant over my children. Josephs, parents was not happy with our decision however, we proceeded with our wedding plans. Our wedding was weird due to the fact, I have no family in fact, my mother poisoned everyone against me so only his family was there we both had friends there. Of course, his parents started asking a lot of questions also, even though I told them about my life, they still wanted to know where my parents and family was.. That was one of the most embarrassing thing I had to deal with, was trying to explain to people that I never had a mother in my current everyday life, or explain that my father is a brittle alcoholic, or that my brother and I are estranged.

However, on the few occasions that I did communicate with my brother he was rude and always disrespectful in fact, my brother was always on my mothers side and he really did not like me very much this is how our relationship has been all our lives. As a result, this is the ingredients for a disastrous wedding. After, we were married Joseph became very controlling slowly, and the verbal abuse started, I could not understand how a man who was so sweet, a man who would take me out to eat dinner, take me for rides in the car, and just having fun could become so selfish and self-centered. Unfortunately, when I was eight months pregnant Joseph became physically abusive he went as far as beating me in the street, and in front of the neighbors. One day, while beating me I ran outside hoping to get help, you see Joseph was 6'5" tall and weighed about 300 pounds however, no one offered to help they were just looking at us as if it was a TV show. In fact, my poor little daughter was running hysterically from house to house knocking on doors begging someone to help me. Finally, someone called the police and the police rolled up on him beating me.

Thank God, he was arrested on the spot, I was admitted into the hospital and his mother cuss me out because her son had to stay in jail over the weekend. This was a Friday night when he came home from work high and drunk after hanging out with his trucker buddies. In fact, not one time or to this day did his parents asked me how I was doing or called to check on my pregnancy or my condition. Finally, our daughter was born my labor was very complicated and long better yet, the baby weighed 10 pounds and 7 ounces at birth. However, she was so beautiful also, she had a head full of curly hair with a beautiful Indian complexion. Joseph, was male chauvinistic and believe that only the mother was supposed to care for the baby only there for, I was the only caregiver for the baby in spite, of my medical condition. Unfortunately, I had no help or support from my husband. A few months after the baby was born I found out Joseph was doing drugs with his trucker buddies which altered his personality tremendously.

Joseph's drug problem became out of control he would demand that I give him my paycheck. After, the baby was a few months old I started working on the weekends I was called the 16 hour girl. Joseph insisted in controlling all the money flow. On his payday after, he would buy his drugs he would then go clothes shopping only for himself, buy food only for himself, and the rest of the money he would spend partying. As a result, everything was slowly turned off the phone, the gas, the water, and electricity Joseph was not paying any utility bills. Therefore, I stopped giving him my paycheck. Every payday there was a loud verbal physical confrontation over my paycheck. Then, he started stealing my car however, he would not even bring my car home in time for me to go to work also, with no gas in it. However, his controlling nature became worse I was not allowed to park in the driveway, he would padlock the bedroom door, I was not allowed in the bedroom until he came home from work which was around seven or eight at night. So, I removed all of my things out of the bedroom and put them in the hall closet also, I've started sleeping on the living room couch.

By now, I have decided to go back to school however, when I told Joseph about my plans to return back to school he became very angry and told me you need to work and forget about going back to school. Nevertheless, I registered for college anyway behind his back unfortunately, his decision did not change infact, he told me when you get your check from college I want it. Besides, I did not listen to him when I got my tuition check from college I took my children shopping for new clothes and shoes, purchased all my books and supplies, then went grocery shopping. When, that fool found out I spent the money he went ballistic and tore up all my expensive books, he put all of my school supplies in his car. Immediately, I called the police and told them what happened when the police arrived Joseph answered the door and told the police to come in. After, the police came in my husband told them look at this place she did this and pointed to me. However, the police believed him. Indeed, he fabricated the truth also, he is a habitual liar with a imaginative imagination. Of course, the police questioned me and I told them the truth however, there was no reason to arrest me but, they gave me a firm warning after the police left the house he laughed so hard and said, you see you can't call the police on me however, that next time you do I'm going to kick your fucking ass, and the next school check you get I want it, then he threw a glass of beer in my face.

Eventually, I left him and filed for divorce. Joseph, stole all of the furniture, appliances, and all of the outside equipment I needed to keep the yard in tact in fact, he even stole the barbecue grill. Our divorce was stressful and drawn out. After, my divorce was final I enrolled in college. Attending college and caring for my children was not easy also, I was working full time. While, on spring break I found out my daughter was pregnant at 15. So while in college full time, working full time, I also had to make time for doctors visits, and a new baby. College, was very hard in fact, I hardly saw my children Sunday was prayer Day and study day finally, I graduated making the Dean's list and merit roll the whole time I was in college.

After, college I started a new job. Generally, I stay to myself, people like to start mess. However, at work a new employee by the name of Angel was just hired to work with me. As a result, we clicked. Working, together was fun, one night after work Angel and I hung out. Angel loved to party and the more the merrier. My first experience of drinking beer was when I started hanging with Angel. Before meeting Angel I lived a boring life in fact, I was in my 30's and had never drank liquor or smoke cigarette. Angel and I did everything together. We went on double dates, shopping, eating out, hanging out at Angels favorite bar, and every Sunday night we went to the disco. Disco dancing was so much fun, not to mention dancing was one of my favorites past times in which I did very well. No matter, what new dance was out, I could do it. Sometimes, while dancing, people would crowd around me just to watch me dance that's how good I was.

Meeting Angel, came at a unique time in fact, I was burned out dealing with all the drama my oldest daughter was involved in. There wasn't a day that went by that did not involve some kind of drama. Certainly, my oldest daughter was constantly in trouble at school. When, I would arrive home from work there was always a neighbor waiting for me to complain about my oldest daughter. Before, I met Angel there was no excitement in life for me. Angel and I were certainly an odd couple in friendship. Angel had long blonde hair with ocean blue eyes but, could not dance a lick. Myself, was a dark Brazilian complexion with shoulder length black hair. As a result, we would attract a lot of attention especially, from men. Of all races nevertheless, Angel told me to stay away from all white men however, she did not take her same advice when it came to dating black men.

One day, Angel insisted that I meet her parents. As a result, Angel brought me home nevertheless, it wasn't the invitation I expected. As soon, as I walked into Angel's parents home her father said I know you... did not bring a nigger in my house. Immediately, I went outside to the car while Angel and her father started to argue. To my surprise Angel defended her friendship with me to her father therefore, I felt as if she was a loyal friend. Of course, my oldest daughter was extremely jealous of our relationship. However, my oldest daughter would do anything negative for my attention nevertheless, her reckless behavior was upsetting to me.

Nevertheless, I refused to let my daughters reckless behavior interfere with my new found friend. Finally, I was enjoying myself. Upon, hanging out with Angel I found out that she loved to date black men although, this was a secret she kept from her family. Of course, Angel did not want me to get involved with white men at all. Not, that I was interested in them although, they were interested in me. For some reason Angel did not like that. Continuing with our friendship there were times I did not agree with everything Angel did. Sometimes, while on lunch breaks Angel always wanted to hit the bar. On break, one particular day Angels car slid into a ditch therefore, we were very late coming back from lunch break. Again, another day while on lunch Angel and I was involved in an car accident. Thank God, it wasn't her fault. As a result, we were rushed to the emergency room.

Angel was worried and suggested that we consult an attorney. Eagerly, I told Angel about my personal attorney who was wonderful. My attorney Johnson and Associates has always been there for me over a period of 20 years therefore, we gave my attorney a call. As a result, some months later our claim was settled. As usual, my attorney came through with flying colors. Financially, we were in good standing. Of course, we went shopping. I treated myself to a new sewing machine also, I treated my kids to close and shoes. Then we went grocery shopping. Angel, had a birthday coming up so I threw her a party at my house. There were lots of delicious foods to eat, liquor, a keg of beer which was Angels idea she loved beer and, ice cream and cake. This seemed like the perfect ingredients for a party however, I had the worse time of everyone at the party. After all, my male friend at the time was cheating on me outside of my house drunk while everyone was inside partying. Angel was so drunk that she passed out on the couch and, the neighbors kids found Angels shoes in their front yard.

Unfortunately, over time Angel and my relationship was slowly slipping away. In fact, there was a lot of constructive criticism from our coworkers concerning our friendship. We were, employed at a predominantly black job site. Nevertheless, I would not let anyone mistreat Angel under any circumstances because, when I am your friend I will be there for you through thick and thin. However, I was not treated in the same fashion from Angel. Angel's family was wealthy to me. They owned their own farm and slaughtered all of their meat in fact, I had never eaten fresh meat before. I, must say it was delicious, tender, and flavorful. Our problem between our relationship was Angel, expected me to attend all of her family functions knowing how raciest they were.

Every year, Angels family would have a pig roast out in Tonto walkis country. There is not a black person within 150 miles yet, and still Angel insisted I be there. Angel was not concerned at all about my safety. Not only was she not concerned about my safety, Angel also wanted me to drive there all by myself also, stay all night with over 200 prejudice white people. Of course, I must say THIS hurt my feelings. I would never have even suggested anything that would have put Angel in danger. And, to this day Angel still do not understand my feelings, and still expects me to visit places that is not safe for me eventually, our relationship went downhill.

A few years later, I asked Angel to be in my wedding. Surprising, I decided to marry again. It was like old times again between Angel and myself. Over the years, I talked a lot about Angel and all the fun we had therefore, I was eager to introduce Angel to my fiancé. Angel, was eager to assist me with my wedding plans also, I felt comfortable with Angel because she knew all about my history with my mother and family. Finally it was my wedding day. Everyone, looked wonderful, our colors were royal blue and silver. Most, of the flowers arrangement and also some of the women accessories were made by me. Nevertheless, I must say I really appreciated Angel sharing my happy day with me.

Off and on, during the years Angel and I stayed in touch, however, I did not find out about Angel's marriage until I accidentally ran into her at the store five years later upon our reunion Angel bragged about her two children and husband and asked if I would come over to meet her family. So, Eagerly, I went to meet Angels husband and children. Upon, my arrival Angel asked me not to mention anything about her involvement with black men. You know, it's funny how people change. Angel was nice and nasty towards me. Somehow, I felt as if Angel was looking down on me as if I wasn't worthy or measured up to her current lifestyle. Again, Angel insisted I spend the night. Also, Angel expected me to get drunk with her husband and his friends either way I would drive drunk or spend the night in a all white highly prejudiced neighborhood in fact, I had reservations driving over there in the afternoon let along driving at night. Unfortunately, I ended our friendship for good.

During this time, I was trying to regroup. Rapidly I grow weary of negative people also, tired of tolerating men. Finally, I was happy to see my daughter enjoying herself with her friends. Neither, did I know I was being plotted against. This time, it was in a positive way. Unaware, that my daughters friend was trying to find a way to tell me about her uncle Gilbert. However, I was not aware that I had an admirer. One day, Gilbert developed enough nerves to ask me if he could sit outside on the porch with me at night, or watch television some time. At this time, I was not interested in starting a romantic friendship. But, this did not stop him from trying to pursue me at all costs. Even though he was nice I decided not to get involved right now.

Therefore, He, would surprise me by taking care of my yard work when I wasn't home. As a result, Gilbert introduced me to his mother who just happen to be an professional baby sitter therefore, we became better acquainted which led to his mom watching my kids. When, Gilbert and I began to date his mother became very resentful towards me, although, she did not let this interfere with her money. By now, Gilbert's mother just tolerated me, you could tell that I wasn't one of her favorite people. As a result, I would send my older daughter to pick up her sister and pay Gilberts mother. After all, I tried to avoid being around his mother.

As time went on I began to look for someone else to look after my kids after school. After, a three-week search I found someone. Even though Gilberts niece and my daughter were still the best of friends this put a strain on Gilberts friendship with me sense his mother was upset about losing the babysitting job. In spite, of the way Gilberts mother felt he would still take care of all my yard work as well. As our friendship progressed Gilberts mother would call consistently on the phone for him. Also, his mother would come over to my house and bang on the door yelling Gilbert you come home right now. Gilbert, was over 35 years old with a receding hair line and grey hair which he would keep shaved bald but, his mother treated him as if he was a child. Unfortunately, this situation was turning me off concerning Gilbert nevertheless, Gilbert pursued me even more than ever.

Therefore, Gilbert continued to visit me after work, and on my days off however, this did not stop his mother. She would send messages through his niece. By now, Gilbert was tired of his mother embarrassing him so, he moved out of his mother's home. Now, we had time to get to know each other better and I must say he was quite the handy man. Gilbert helped me move. Also, he put all the furniture in place, after, he helped me clean the carpet or any other needs I had. Of course, his mother was plotting against us in fact, she found out where I moved to from his niece. Unfortunately, I was not aware of his drinking problem. Whenever, Gilbert would visit he was always on his best behavior of course, he would have some beers from time to time. Gilbert's, mother knew about his weakness which was 100 proof Brandy.

Therefore, every payday Gilberts mother would have a card party with a gallon of brandy on the table. After all,

I wasn't aware that Gilbert being with me was cutting off his mothers bill and food money. As a result, his mother had found a way to get her money back. Every week, there was a card party with his sisters and brothers impatiently I would sit and wait until the game was over. After, Gilbert was drunk and broke suddenly the card game was over. Everyone, would be up and gone from the table before Gilbert realized that his whole paycheck was gone, they did not even leave him a penny or a crumb. That's when I told him to go where his money was because, he wasn't going home with me broke and drunk. Of course, I found this to be very disturbing in fact, I told him that this type of behavior could not continue if he planned on being with me. Nevertheless, Gilbert was tired of being broke therefore, he straightened up his act for a while.

For a while, things was going better at lease Gilbert was trying to make our relationship work. Better yet, Gilberts mother was cooking up some more schemes. This time, his mother called his ex-wife and told her about our relationship and insisted that his two kids move in with her stating that they need to be close to their father. As a result, things did not work out exactly how his mother planned them to therefore, Gilberts mother told his ex-wife where I lived also, his mother told his ex-wife that Gilbert was not spending time with his kids. To make a long story short Gilberts ex-wife was not happy with the new arrangement concerning the kids in fact, she was upset about her child support money as well. Gilbert would not pay her while the children was staying with his mother. And his mother knew this however, his mother was getting what she wanted Gilbert's money.

As time went on things seemed to work themselves out. Gilbert and I was becoming closer. Every night, Gilbert was over we spent a lot of time together cooking, watching TV, going shopping, visiting our friends, and eating out. Eventually, Gilbert and I decided to get married at this time I asked Gilbert how are you going to tell your mother about our plans to get married. Gilbert replied, don't worry I will take care of it therefore I continue to make our wedding plans. At the time, I was employed by the sisters of Charity. So, Gilbert and myself talked with the priest at my job eagerly farther John was happy to marry us also, father John gave us pre marriage counseling. On that day of our wedding Gilbert told me he had a special surprise for me concerning his family. Finally, I was happy that his family would be attending the services or I think that's what the surprise is.

Father John, made our wedding day special also, our wedding ceremony was on all the patients TV. Everyone, witnessed our marriage except Gilberts family. The surprise was on me Gilbert was lying the whole time concerning his family there was no surprise in fact, his family stated that they heard that we were getting married but, did not believe it. Nevertheless, we went away for a few days after, we returned home both of us visited Gilberts mother. Gilbert's mother, was very angry about our marriage better yet, Gilbert's mother looked me directly in the face and told him you can always come home if things are not working out. You do not have too stay married to her. One week later, after I left for work my daughter called me up at work at about 6:00 AM screaming that she had saw a mouse immediately, I said where's Gilbert my daughter said he is gone.

While, on both of my breaks I went home to check on my daughter. After work, Gilbert still was not home therefore, I went looking for him finally, I found him or shall I say I found his car parked in front of one of his single friends house. Upon, discovering his car my anger overcame me. At this time, I got out of my car popped my hood removed my crowbar out of the trunk and busted out all of the windows in his car. Unfortunately, after that the marriage was over however, I do not regret busting out his car windows because Gilbert was a step father and was wrong to leave my daughter at home alone, at the time my youngest daughter was eight years old her sisters were at a teenage sleepover.

Congratulations, to Gilberts mother. She won the fight. Things, was not working out there for, Gilbert moved back home with his mother however, I would never trust him with my daughter again anyway. Did I mention, when he left he stole one of my cars to replace the one I destroyed. While the car was in his custody Gilbert did not make any payments which lead to my filing bankruptcy to keep my wages from being garnished. Over a decade had passed however, I never saw Gilbert again. One day, while at work I overheard a patient talking about a friend of her son that was diagnosed with HIV. During, her conversation with another patient she said he had contracted it from his next-door neighbor who had already passed on. I regret to inform you that the friend of her son was my ex-husband Gilbert. Gilbert's mother did not want him with anyone. She was a very selfish woman. Now, she has her son also, now she has to watch him die...

CHAPTER

NINE

At this time, my older daughter was out of control constantly suspended from school for fighting. However, the fights were becoming more and more malicious to the point of retaliations on other peoples houses and property which involved the police. Every day, when I would arrive home from work there were neighbors, parents, or the police waiting to talk to me concerning my daughter. All my lunch breaks were spent coming home to check on my house and my daughter. One day, I came home to check on the house and my daughter however, she was undressed with a boy in the house that she tried to hide but, I sniffed him out, then I beat him down the stairs and out the door with a base ball bat. Trying, to work and keep up with my daughter, her sisters, and the upkeep of a house was starting to take a toll on me. Eventually, our arguments became very explosive to the point of me telling my daughter that her father raped me. I was angry because after he ruined my life he ran off and stuck me with all the responsibility of raising her after he was discharged from the Air Force I did not receive any more child support from him.

This is something I've always regretted saying but now I can't take it back. As a result, my daughter became more out of control she started abusing her sisters, more rebellious, still constantly fighting and cutting school. My daughter knew the history between myself and my mother in fact, she would play us against each other. My daughter was very spiteful and whenever she would get angry she would do something really big to start some mess for example, she knew I did not want my mother to know where I live however, she told my mother were I live also, she gave her my phone number after that, the crank calls started. While, at work I received a phone call from my younger daughter stating that when she arrived home from school someone had wrote bad names profanity in white chalk all over the side of my house. Of course, my older daughter swore she did not do it. After, investigating the matter, and talking to the police, and neighbors I found out it was my mother the description the neighbors gave me was of her.

Unfortunately, my house was brown and after several washings you could still see the bad names that was written on the house. Again, I had to change my phone number. Finally, my mother had came out of hiding and all the horrible things started all over again. At income tax time we moved again, I sent my oldest daughter to stay with her father I could not go on with the constant fighting between her and her sisters, she was failing in school, there were also constant attacks on my house because of her enemies, my daughter and my relationship was destructive. When she went to live with her father she started a lot of trouble between him and his fiancée, not to mention she became pregnant while under his care.

I am not sorry that things went the way they did between my daughter and her father. For, 16 years I had sole custody of our daughter, and the one time he has to deal with her is a problem. Besides, what upsets me the most is he created this situation in fact, I was only 14 years old but, I stood up and handled my business also, I feel that anything that happens to Dennis he deserves. The one thing that gets me the most, is he wants to be looked up to in society as someone important. The last I heard, Dennis is employed as a teacher for elementary children when in all reality he is a rapist, a liar, a hypocrite, and physically and verbally abusive. Of course, he doesn't want anyone to know this in his current lifestyle. Therefore, Dennis sent our daughter to my mother without my knowledge. You see they were close and in constant communication with each other. After all, this time I thought my daughter was in Georgia with her father when all the time she was with my mother. Again, Dennis dodged his responsibilities again. My mother hired an attorney to take me to court for custody and child support of my daughter that is how I found out that she was with my mother.

As a result, I still don't understand to this day why do people do things that's wrong but, do not want anyone to know about it. If, you know what you are doing is wrong why, do you do it. However, I do know one thing anyone who throw a rock and hide is a dirty coward. Dennis ruined my life then stuck me with all the responsibility of raising her. I hate him so much. When I asked Dennis why he raped me he stated that he was extremely sexually attracted to me but, I wanted nothing to do with him at all in fact, I despised him also, he knew that I was in love with Marvin. Also, Dennis knew that my mother did not care about me at all therefore, he knew that he would get away with it and, he did. Dennis should have been arrested and prosecuted for what he did to me, I was only 14 years old. He has a lot of nerve to pretend as if he hasn't done anything to me. The beatings were compulsive, he would start beating me with his hands, then he would lift up the mattress to get a bed slack to beat me with, after that he would go to the closet, get a clothes hanger disassemble it then he would beat me with it. After, he was done with the whole episode which sometimes was over an hour rampage. To this day Dennis acts as if it was nothing. Also, Dennis has not apologized to me for all of the extreme intense chronic beatings I had to endure while, my mother watched. Every day, all my life I was in extreme danger.

However, looking back at my journey, I don't know how I made it through. My journey was very difficult and long which last for four years. Pursuing my education was not easy. Unfortunately, I was forced to drop out of school in the 10th grade because, I was not allowed to go out of the house. Most of the time I was so badly bruised from the beatings I did not want anyone to see me like this. To this day I have problems with trusting men. Over the years this situation has caused me mental pain and suffering every day I relive every thing sometimes, I suffer with nightmares and flashbacks. Nevertheless, I did return back to school starting with the 10th grade. You see, I did not want a GED certificate. I wanted a diploma. As a result, I achieved my goal graduating and receiving a diploma. However, there was no one at my graduation to cheer me on. I just think God for giving me the courage to finish school.

CHAPTER

TEN

Throughout, this journey I ran so much in my life I literally wore out my feet resulting in 5 foot surgeries.

To this day I've never had a good man, not even a decent man. After all, I grow weary of tolerating men. On my journey, I met several snakes. Some situations I was in was terrifying. Every day, I knew only God and prayer could get me out of them. My relationship with my older daughter is destroyed. In fact, my other two daughters do not want anything to do with their sister. She has caused a lot of problems for her sisters while my middle daughter was pregnant her sister told her fiancée whole family that her sister was cheating on him and that the baby was not his also, she went over to her sisters apartment while she was pregnant and attacked her with a hatchet also, destroying all her furniture then, she called children services on her sister which almost resulted in her losing her children. My younger daughter was also a victim the last time she was in the company of her older sister she cut off all of her hair every day, my youngest daughter would wear a bandanna she would sleep in it as well however, one day I asked her why she was wearing a bandanna every day she replied, it's the style right now all of the kids are wearing them at school. Unfortunately, one morning I went into her room to get her up for school and that's when I found out that her older sister had cut off all of her hair she was trying to keep this a secret from me.

To this day, I still don't have a relationship with either of my brothers unfortunately, Alex suffers with schizophrenia, and deterioration of the brain in fact, he do not know any of his family members including me which was a mother figure for him. Howard, and myself are estranged. I have no clue where he lives I just know that he lives somewhere in Columbus Ohio. To this day, I have never had the opportunity to meet his only son which is probably about 25 years old or older. This is what happens when you raise one child to be superior over another. As a result, it's sad how two people my mother and Dennis has destroyed so many lives. To this day, my mother still will not admit to the things she did to me. All the torment, psychological, mental, physical and verbal abuse I endured, 60% of most of my problems in life was caused by my mother in fact, I waited 30 years hoping, praying that she would be women enough to come clean to my family members, my brother, my children, and myself however, Howard knew I was being abused by our mother.

Unfortunately, the truth would never be told, my mother was diagnosed with Alzheimer's disease which resulted in memory loss. Nevertheless, all these years the only thing my mother was concerned about was her own reputation with no regard on how others viewed me, what a selfish act. To this day I have never once disrespected, cursed or was rude to my mother never. Again, why do people do things that is wrong but, do not want anyone to know about it. Every time, I would tell people the truth they would not believe me because my mother had enough sense not to do horrible things to me in front of her friends and family members in fact, if someone would tell my mother what I said about her, she would deny it yelling that's a lie I would never do anything like that to my only daughter which is THE UNTOLD SECERTS.'

Destruction of our children begins in the home when

the mother or the father or a sibling physically, mentally, verbally or sexually abuse their children or sibling.

This is a private war that is taking place all over America, Which, "is a well kept secret."

This war affects our schools, our communities, and countries all over the world.

Charity starts at home and spread abroad.

When a child is degraded in their home where they are suppose to feel safe and secure.. Our children becomes mentally pledged with destruction because, they do not feel good about themselves.

Which, results in a circle of negativity. Children attacking back on their parents, siblings, classmates, and neighborhood.

With a quality of low self image.

This is not a black problem, or a white problem, or a Hispanic problem, or a problem of any race. Abuse is orchestrated from all walks of life. Also, it has become a rising problem all over America affecting teachers who are responsible for educating our children.

Our, teen girls lack respect for their bodies. Instead of focusing on education and career goals they are becoming pregnant, in gangs, or dropping out of school.

Our, teen boys listen to gangster rap and play mentally destructive video games that degrades the mind at a time when they should be focused on education, career goals and, spreading the back bone to become structured in fulfilling the responsibility of hard work, with pride and dignity in becoming a proud citizen in society.

Without, proper structure and guidance we have ignorance, graffiti Art on our buildings and schools. Gang wars and a population of individuals who lack determination and respect for their current surroundings.

Currently, I am still employed as a dialysis technician. Sewing, will always be my first love and every chance I get I make myself something beautiful. However, swimming, is my second love you see, I was afraid of large bodies of water, astonishingly I conquered my fear of water now I go swimming two days a week also, I do aqua aerobics as well. My third love is making jewelry a coworker of mine taught me how to make jewelry and three weeks later I had mastered the art and within a month I was selling jewelry to everyone with all satisfied customers. I reside in a prestigious suburb. My daughters are doing fine. I am happy to say that all of my daughters are employed, and living well. Unfortunately, at this time I am off work with a hip injury which gave me time to write this book. Every day, unfortunately I carry around a demon behind my knee its called a Baker's cyst. However, I've been to over several doctors and none of them would remove the cyst. Drs. would rather do a knee replacement, or heart surgery than remove a Baker's cyst. Which is an out patient procedure that takes only 30 minutes or less.

To prove my point I had knee surgery the doctor said I had a torn meniscus however, during the surgery which was the same knee that the cyst was in however, my doctor left the cyst behind my knee after he had opened my knee for surgery did whatever he had to do then, closed up my knee. After, surgery my Baker's cyst became worse the surgery aggravated the cyst so now I suffer even more with it considering I've had it for 13 years and I pray every day that I will find a doctor to remove it. In the meantime the cyst has to be drained whenever it becomes inflamed and full of fluid. Fortunately, for me I found a compassionate caring physician who takes care of this problem for me.

Six years ago I was diagnosed with a disease called Sarcodosis which fight against your own immune system. Currently, I am adjusting to the disease and learning what to do concerning this disease. And out of all the the issues I endure I never missed a day of work or made excuses for it. I just pray to God to take me through another day.

Nevertheless, myself or my two daughters do not have a relationship with my oldest daughter, there is too much damage done also, the trusts is gone for ever. My oldest and my middle daughters both have two children. My youngest daughter has no kids and has moved out, and for a while we were not on speaking terms because she dropped out of school two months before graduation and while running the streets during school time the truant officer picked her up which resulted in a warrant put out for my arrest because, she cut school. My youngest daughter disappointed me. Unfortunately, I never saw any of my daughters graduate my two oldest daughters both has GED's and I was looking forward to seeing my youngest daughter graduate. That's why, I was working full-time and attending college full time to set an example for them however, this did not make a difference to my daughter in fact, my daughter told me just because you went to college doesn't mean I want to go to college. Amen. As a result, there was no reason for her to remain under my care. In life you must pursue your education to accomplish your goals in life. In all reality there is no reason for her not to finish school. This was one of the most disappointing situations in life for me. However, to my amazement she went back to school and achieved a GED certificate working at a prestigious hospital, in college, and has her own apartment doing wonderful also, my oldest daughter has changed and is very talented also, has her own business and, she takes care of homeless children. I am very proud of her. It wasn't her fault how she came into the world. Indeed, she was a victim as well. As a result, she was just hurting inside. However, through Gods grace she over come her battles.

CHAPTER

ELEVEN

Therefore, after you go through all the pain and suffering of raising children without the fathers emotional, physical, and financial support. When all is said and done and they are all grown up doing fine productive citizens in society then, the absent father comes out of the woodwork and take all the credit for all the hard work I have done in fact, you should see how their fathers brag and show off their daughters to friends and family members. This is my child. I, resent this because it was hard raising them without any kind of support at all at one time we were homeless and we stayed in a house with no electricity, no water, no gas, and no phone in fact, I used to catch water into garbage cans so we could//flush the toilet, I, used a torch so that we could see how to get dressed, I had to go food shopping daily, everything was cooked outside on a barbecue grill. At night, we would watch our battery operated television for only one hour so that we would not use up the batteries so fast. However, I worked at a nursing home and I would sneak and wash my kids clothes and dry them also, I would fold them very neatly, because I had no way of ironing them.

We, would go to the recreation center and shower and wash our hair. At night, when it was cold all of us would sleep together with coats, blankets, and clothes to stay warm also, we had a battery operated alarm clock to wake us up in the morning however, the only communication we had was the corner payphone. The children did their homework by candlelight. This is why I resent their fathers eagerness to take the credit for all the hard work I've done. Getting, on with my life was an adjustment nevertheless, I managed to always land on my feet. Over the years, I wanted to find Marvin. Therefore, I looked up his sisters phone number.

Unfortunately, his sister was not happy to hear from me. She was bitter and stated that I had ruined her brothers life therefore, I did not try to pursue him again. Nevertheless, my children felt that it was unhealthy for me to hold on to the memories I harbor for Marvin. They did not want me to go through the pain and agony of holding on to something that would never be. Even though, I told my kids the stories of how we met also, how much I still loved him. Besides, my children wanted me to move closer to them so that I would not be so lonely therefore, some, years later I decided to buy my own home and my son-in-law heard an advertisement on the radio about buying homes, so he called the radio station and gave them my phone number there for, an agent phoned me concerning this matter. However, the agent and myself started to look for homes but during the time we spent together a romance started. While dating the real estate agent told me he was a pastor of a church also, and invited me to attend.

When, I started dating the pastor I had been single and celibate for over four years so, I stressed to him that our relationship would have to be serious and important eventually leading towards marriage. After, dating for some time he asked me to marry him and stated that he was making regular payments on an engagement ring for me. I really thought the pastor was sincere after all, I met his only son and his mother in fact, we would sit together in church also, he told my children, his mother, my friends and his friends about our upcoming engagement however, we did not tell the church we decided we would tell them after we were married because it would not look right for the pastor to have a unmarried relationship with a member of the church. At last, I thought I had found a good man, or better still a God sent man. I really thought the pastor was serious about our commitment to each other The pastor put me on a pedestal. I was showered with gifts, balloons, clothes, and taken on holidays almost every weekend. He would clean my apartment, do my laundry, and do all my grocery shopping. Every night, when I would arrive home from work my dinner would be cooked, my bath water ran, and a drink waiting for me. The pastor felt extremely comfortable with me therefore, he would share all the details of his life with me. Even though the pastor spoiled me rotten I could see how he treated other people. The pastor was very verbally abusive towards his mother. In fact, it would make me sick to my stomach every time I would hear him curse at her. Nevertheless, I felt as if I was selling my soul to the devil.

Later on, in our relationship I received a phone call from a woman stating that she also was the pastors fiancé and that she had got my phone number out of his phone while he was sleeping after they had sex. Out of all the relationships I've had in my life I never had a woman call me concerning my partner until I dated a pastor. Dating, a pastor I have more problems than dating a regular person. I trusted and believed he was a man of his word and a faithful servant of the Lord. In all reality, I never would have expected this behavior from a pastor also, he is a big liar. I expected him to be someone to look up to and respect, someone to follow and guide me in the right direction in life. However, on my journey with the pastor he would constantly disrespect the commandments of God without a conscience which is despicable. I found out he was a con man, a liar, a cheater, he was deceitful, verbally and physically abusive when angered. So I exit the relationship and the church. I am quite sure things would have changed after we were married.

Also, he was a womanizer, and controlling. He listens to gangster rap and I mean X-RATED. The Pimp gangster lifestyle fascinate him and, he refuses to give it up. He is like Clark Kent from Monday to Friday, Saturday he studies the Bible for Sunday sermon. Saturday night, he would call you and say I'm going to bed early I have to be fresh for church in the morning then he would hang up the phone get dressed and go see his other woman sometimes he would oversleep and be late for Sunday school. Then, he would put on his church robe and deceive and brainwash the congregation. Also, he has two personalities one is the pastor and good man image, the other personality is a demon however, the demon personality is rapidly taking over and he finds it hard to resist his temptations. I actually, watched him revolve from one personality to the other. He is a fake full servant of the Lord you can not serve two masters, so far he is doing it faithfully.

The pastor, use the church as a front to gain respect from every day people and the congregation. He is living his life breaking every commandment against God in fact, he would get up every Sunday and preach the gospel as if he was a perfect servant of the Lord. Of course, there are wonderful prestigious representatives for God. However, pastors like this gives the whole ministry association a bad name, and makes it hard for people to trust. The journey to lead people to God is hard enough. Because of my involvement with the pastor my children does not want any thing to do with me, and they don't even know the whole truth about him. You see, my kids are very protective of me in fact, in their eyes there is no one that is good enough.

Unfortunately, for the pastor his pimp gangster lifestyle has come to an abrupt end. When, he was charged with aggravated menacing, kidnapping, and possession of a firearm and assault on his new live-in lover. However, the pastor feels he will be vindicated. However, I have never seen this side of him.

Do to all the stress of the trial the pastor suffered a stroke.

Nevertheless, he has torn down the religious trust of all his followers. Also, he has created a spiritual mess of the House of God. In fact, I would think this charge would carry an bigger sentence with God than the one man can give you. because vindication starts *with the heart. One must change his heart and humble his spirit in order to change. As well, one must confess the wrong he has done.*

Also, you must be prepared to serve two sentences. The one man gives you and, the one God gives you. The sentence man gave him is nine years in prison...

Over the years I've cried enough tears to fill an ocean

All, my life I was nothing but a victim.

All, I did wrong, my only fault was thinking I could feel safe in my own home.

Some, of my involvements, I was wrong.

I, made that mistake, by mixing business with pleasure.

You, can't mix business with pleasure.

In fact, I insulted my own intelligence by doing this.

Do not, lower yourself to someone else's standards that can't rise to yours.

You, will find out what's up, when you are down.

God will always Send a messenger ahead of you to prepare you for what is in front of you.

CHAPTER

TWELVE

In life, you must know that, when the ball is in your court, you must play the game. Take advantage of a situation that is in your favor. Also, pray for wisdom and knowledge so you will be able to see beyond horizons. Life is like a Spy Movie with espionage and terror, and you are captured and trapped by terrorists, but all of a sudden there is a way out and you take it. You run with all your might to save your life, you run for safety, this is how life is.

When, God gets you out of a bad situation, keep walking straight and don't look back in spite of the devils temptations for nothing, because you will turn into a pillar of salt. Which means, you will be destroyed. Your life, will be a living hell. Always, exit a bad situation when God gives you a out also, he will protect you as well from the enemy. And, when you meet people who are in a bad and negative situation in life do not get involved, stay out of other people affairs. Then, say to yourself this is your nightmare not mines, and I choose not to be in it. If, you are in a bad situation that look like there is no way out, just pray. There is hope when it seems like there is no way out. Also, Please, please, pray and trust in God, he will guide you also, he will always create a diversion to exit you out of a crisis.

HOWEVER, I have found that you have to make your time on earth mean something. You, must
Have something to show for all your pain and suffering.
Don't, let anyone take anything from you
That you have earned, and that you deserve. Therefore, do not give up on your dreams, constantly
Pray and ask for God's mercy. Never, be afraid to choose a different future. Always, fight for

What you believe in, and most of all, always, always
believe in yourself.
Never break bread with your enemies.
Never change horses in the middle of a race. You, will
never win.
When, two people love each other it doesn't matter, how
many years that is between us. It, doesn't
Matter how many addresses. It doesn't matter how many
people or phone numbers we've found or
Lost. The only thing that matters is the love still remains
in your heart for ever. When, you
Experience falling in love nothing feels the same, food
doesn't taste the same, music doesn't sound the
Same.
Until, one day a glance, a smile, and suddenly life is
alive. However, without love earth can be such
A sad and lonely place.

THE END